Empires and Holy Lands

MICHAEL HULSE was born in 1955 and grew up in Stoke-on-Trent. He read German at the University of St. Andrews and has taught English and post-colonial literature at universities in Germany and Switzerland. His poetry has earned him numerous awards and taken him on reading tours worldwide, and his work as a translator (Goethe, Wassermann, Sebald) has been widely praised. He runs the poetry press, Leviathan, and edits *Leviathan Quarterly*.

Empires and Holy Lands

Poems 1976–2000

Michael Hulse

SALT

PUBLISHED BY SALT PUBLISHING
PO Box 202, Applecross, Western Australia 6153
PO Box 937, Great Wilbraham, Cambridge PDO CB1 5JX United Kingdom

© Michael Hulse, 2002

The right of Michael Hulse to be identified as the
author of this work has been asserted by him in accordance
with Section 77 of the Copyright, Designs and Patents Act 1988.

First published 2002

Printed and bound in the United Kingdom by Lightning Source

Typeset in Swift 9.5 / 13

ISBN 1 876857 46 3 paperback

SP

1 3 5 7 9 8 6 4 2

This book is for

Charles
David
Greg
John
Karl
three Peters
Robert
and Vincent

fellow labourers in the vineyard

Contents

Acknowledgements

The previously collected poems in this book were chosen from *Knowing and Forgetting* (Secker and Warburg, 1981): 'Knowing', 'Rotterdam, 07.50, December 22nd', 'Dole Queue', 'Europe', 'The Bell-ringer', 'Village Performance', 'After Rain', 'Twentieth Burning in the Bishopric of Würzburg', 'Festival of Youth', 'Young Mother', 'La Gazzetta', 'Silver Wedding'; from *Propaganda* (Secker and Warburg, 1985): 'Welcome to the Delectable Mountains', 'At Aigues-Mortes', 'Helicopter', 'Evening at Imogiri', 'Brunei', 'A Family Portrait circa 1900', 'The Prisoner', 'Phrenology, 1914', 'On Location', 'One Damn Thing after Another', 'Loreley', 'Windowless Monads', 'Tangle'; and from *Eating Strawberries in the Necropolis* (Harvill, 1991): 'The Country of Pain and Revelation', 'Five Poems after Winslow Homer', 'At Avila', 'Horns', 'Fornicating and Reading the Papers', 'A Chinese Tale', 'Raffles Hotel', 'Nine Points of the Nation', 'Refugees', 'To Botho Strauss in Berlin', 'Roadworkers Picking Cherries', 'To Gottlob Fabian', 'The Architecture of Air', 'Eating Strawberries in the Necropolis', 'Adultery', 'An Aluminium Casket Would be a Good Idea', 'The Evidence of Things Not Seen', 'Concentrating', 'Carnation, Lily, Lily, Rose', 'An American Murder'. The poem 'Mother of Battles' is from the book of that title, published in 1991 by Arc Publications, and the poems 'Homo Sum', 'A Treatise on the Astrolabe' and 'The Critics Are Too Much with Us' are from the pamphlet *Monteverdi's Photographs*, published in 1995 in Australia by Folio (Salt).

The following poems are newly collected in this volume: 'Calcutta Red', 'Simla', 'That Christmas', 'Heathrow', 'Burslem', 'White', 'The Winter Ward', 'The Pointlessness of Poetry', 'The Kid', 'A Sonnet', 'The Yuppie in Love', 'To His Coy Mistress', 'The Sigh', 'There's Something About a Cow', 'Stopping by Woods without a Map', 'The Essential Auden', 'The Thunder and Lightning Poker'. Some of these poems were published in *London Magazine*, *PN Review*, *Poetry Review*, *Quadrant*, *Salt*, *The Spectator*, *The Sydney Morning Herald* and in *One for Jimmy* (Hereford and Worcester County Council, 1992), ed. Matthew Sweeney, *New Writing 5* (Vintage, 1996), ed. Christopher Hope and Peter Porter, and *New Writing 8* (Vintage, 1999), ed. Tibor Fischer and Lawrence Norfolk.

'Dole Queue' won the 1978 National Poetry Competition, 'Raffles Hotel' won the 1988 Bridport poetry competition, and 'The Kid' won the same competition in 1994.

I Empires

Calcutta Red

The day of the rally, I took a car to Kalighat.
Down all the helter-swelter of the city's arteries,
buses and trucks were roaring as fever roars in the blood,
brash, intractable, hot,

scarlet banners wild,
Marx on the glittering grilles,
anger high and red, haranguing, pounding, punching the air,
set to inherit the earth.

The taxi crawled past columns of marchers
come to the city from villages fifty miles off –
incorrigibles, the destitute, the prophets,
the sea-green bright-eyed boys, the no-hope poor –

and turned aside as if turning from the world
in weariness of life.
We drove down dusty streets where heaps of roadside trash
were people's homes, or people,

where unproud houses leaned toward a fall,
and women selling pomegranates
shied a sidewise shame
as if they sold themselves,

one fruit at the top of each tidy pile
sliced open in glistening red,
wet and sexual.
The men spat beteljuice and looked away.

The temple was tucked in a muck of commerce and dreck.
Self-absorbed, in love with death,
it stood apart from all the traffic of survival.
The shrine of Kali. Goddess of the killers.

I walked with a priest in immaculate white
through a mire of worship, a grime of belief.
His weasel grin was leery with secrets,
predatory, sycophantic, lean.

The temple of the city of the dead
was scarlet with hibiscus, basketfuls
of slaughterhouse flowers as red as butchered meat.
I reeled in the heat and reek of dirt and easeful beauty.

How hard he loved his mystery, the priest.
He said his words and smudged my brow with ash.
I sickened at his trash. He seized my wrist
and led me to the place of sacrifice:

a paste of old black blood, buzzing with flies,
a slick of fresh arterial blood,
a puddled slime of goatshit and goatpiss,
splashes of blood up the steps of the prayer hall.

I watched three women walk to the chopping block,
self-possessed, intent, and full of grace,
wearing their sense of purpose as they wore
the gash of married scarlet in their hair.

The women had their blessing and their lust.
Attendants dragged their goats in by the ears.
The goats set up a shrieking as they slithered on the slick,
screaming like children.

And there stood Kali's bloodman, in his spattered singlet,
unceremonial, waiting to do his job,
his abattoir deliberation
gleaming in the sun like the blade of his cleaver.

Simla

They say two senile memsahibs still live here,
colonel's daughters who stayed on into their dotage,
carefully collapsing into British dereliction:
slippage, dementia, smallness.

They say they were wonderful once.
Their bodies were young and fresh and proud.
Their bodies were fragrant of cotton and vanilla.
Willowy. Wily with innocence.

When the colonel's daughters turned in the door
of the viceroy's lodge, to drop their curtseys
under the portraits of Dufferin and Curzon,
the men were a beat in the air, a held breath.

I think of the colonel's daughters dancing under the deodars,
moonlighting, flirting, wanting it all,
the music heard below, in the hillside bazaars,
by Indians who were banished from the Mall.

What am I doing here?
This café was converted from a British army bandstand.
We're sitting on the terrace, Jagdish Bhatt and me,
the city a litter of history below us,

the mountains a jagged white, far off, a glare.
By Christ Church, near the statue of Indira Gandhi,
three vans are parked, marked AMBULANCE,
and a fourth, lettered in red DEAD BODY VAN.

A correspondent for *The Times of India*.
Behind his Ray Bans, irony writes, and writes afresh,
as he talks of covering Himachal Pradesh,
the state where nothing happens any more.

Not that he'd want it back, the summer capital
of garden parties, balls, and Raj adultery,
Gilbert and Sullivan at the Gaiety,
archery at Annandale.

But still, the British got things done.
The trains. The roads. A vision with a map.
When Delhi was laid out anew, the roadside trees
were planted with such foresight, such precision,

that decades and three or four widenings later
there's been no need to fell them yet.
Clerks and police and government did their work
efficiently, politely, and unbribed.

I've heard the argument before. And Jagdish means it all.
It's not a sop to the visiting Brit. But still,
it puts good engineering where good ethics ought to be.
Like praising Hitler's motorways and Mussolini's trains.

Liberal goody-two-shoes that I am,
I want to say that nothing compensates
for robbing a people of their self-esteem,
stripping them of their independent power

to make their lives in ways to suit themselves.
I'd mean it. But I'd be dissatisfied.
It's not the whole truth either. Something stops my mouth.
Our talk is not of history, but how we know our home.

One night I watched the light die over Simla.
Dusk was stroking the town like a hand on a breast.
Lights were starring the landslide of homes on the hills,
and I ached for something I didn't have a name for:

if the colonel's fragrant daughters had been there
I'd have wanted to make a kind of love to them,
as the night came in like a warm and comforting tide
lapping the starry past in a mantle of black.

Raffles Hotel

Singapore

Say a colonial sailed up the straits and saw
a fishing village. And set foot in a city.
        Say the future was opium
        traded for tea, parades on the padang,

secret societies, rickshaws on Collyer Quay,
and riots in the streets. Say an Armenian
        bought the villa where a bankrupt
        colonel had opened a tiffin parlour,

and made a white hotel, a place of colonnades
and frangipani, palms, pilasters, rattan blinds,
        piano waltzes in the court:
        the marriage of the bride to the roué.

And while men died at the Somme and at Passchendaele
a barman was (gently) shaking the first gin sling.
        While General Percival puffed
        and dallied, refusing to fortify

Singapore on the landward side, the Japanese
were riding down the peninsula on bikes. For
        history is a seduction:
        cocktails on the verandah, then dinner

at eight, and the stylish contempt of the waiters.
After the rain the sky is open again. Stars
        are holed in the indigo night.
        A British lord and lady lead their guests

to a private banquet where pipers are playing
"Scotland the Brave". An Australian swears that the
        last tiger killed on the island
        was shot underneath the billiard table.

This is the idiot empire. I'm lapping the
pool past midnight, thinking of Dad, and a jazz band's
      playing in the bar. After the
   war he dealt in textiles in Raffles Place,

and one day his driver came early to warn him
and hurry him to a villa where Englishmen
      waited armed behind shutters all
   the fanatical afternoon and night,

making light of their fears, but whispering, watching,
alert for a palm to sway as these do now, in
      the innocent air, trembling with
   the darker breathing of the saxophone.

Village Performance

after Wang Li-Ping

In a quiet part of Yunnan
Province we live, and now that night
    is drawing its blue blind
down on the world and a thin white
hammock of moon hangs relaxed in
    the nude ultramarine
of pure sky, we have come to stand

on a dun dusty stony patch
where the air is sultry with maize
    and sweat and leafage and
sweet evening, and shake off the day's
desolate sameness. And we watch
    the players, savour each
splendid sweep of a shaping hand,

fist of perfect formulation,
motion of making, of what's made
    with method. The boy in
palest blue shakes thin tintinnades
from his flute, and the nation
    listens, approbation
creating our faces, drawing

directions and desires onto
the human planes of bone and skin.
    The naked bulbs with blue
shades shed light where it belongs, in
the trees loudspeakers hang, and you
    can see and hear it so
well that in the end maybe you

see nothing at all. The cymbals
batter, the drums butt and thump, the
    accordion player
smiles. We love it. When later we
leave on our yellow bicycles,
    past the telegraph poles
and the village dynamo where

the world's pulse throbs dull as thunder,
the hero's heart beats in our breast.
    We too are travellers
with the moon through night to the west,
and one day we will see wonders.
    We ride away, under
the endless pity of the stars.

A Chinese Tale

I dreamt I was the simple trusting boy
who took his wicked teacher's jealous hand
and climbed the mountain. And the teacher said
he had to go away, but he'd be back,
and if I happened to be hungry, why,
all I need do was eat the stones. His eyes
were fine strokes of a calligrapher's brush
conveying messages I could not read
(though how I longed to learn and understand).
I thanked the honest man for his advice
and said that I would wait till he returned.
He told me patience was a discipline
invaluable to a man. And left.

The day was bright, and I was young in hope,
and I questioned the sun, and the sun replied:
Study. Be humble. Be truthful. Aspire.
And I questioned the sky, and the sky replied:
Study. Be humble. Be truthful. Aspire.
And night came, and the ironic moon
replied with a smile: Be truthful. Aspire.
And keep up the studies. Because you know
that all will come to him who learns and waits.
But don't overdo the humility, boy.

And in the morning I was cold and hungry.

And I recalled the honest man's advice
and went about collecting stones, although
I must confess I'd never heard that stones
were good to eat. An inspiration came
and prompted me to warm them on my feet,
and in their place I saw a bowl of rice
and ate of it till I could eat no more.
And I questioned the sun, and the sun replied:
Study. Be humble. Be truthful. Aspire.

And I questioned the sky, and the sky replied:
Study. Be humble. Be truthful. Aspire.
And night came, and the ironic moon
replied with a smile: You're on the right track,
but remember that study's a means, not an end,
and aspiration's the vehicle, not the goal,
and humility may be counter-productive,
and even the truth isn't always the answer.

And in the morning I breakfasted on stones.

And the days went by, the days became weeks,
and, knowing that patience was a virtue
invaluable to a man, I waited,
hourly expecting my honest teacher's return.
And after forty days he did return,
important in his venerable robes,
and seemed surprised to find me still alive.
He listened with a serious expression
as I explained about the stones and rice.
The fine strokes narrowed into finer strokes.
I told him the sun's reply and he smiled.
I told him the sky's reply and he smiled.
I told him the moon's reply and he frowned.

And then it seemed I fell from off the mountain,
uncertain whether I was pushcd, and woke
at daybreak on a square, where people cried
and ran and fell and lay where they had fallen.
And I questioned the rising sun and the sky
but they made no reply.
And I questioned the setting moon and the moon replied:
Today you died.

JUNE 1989

Helicopter

We are leaving them behind, the children,
who played in the dust for butterflies pinned on card,
    for buttons or cartridge cases:
leaving, leaving them all, for faraway places
    with faraway names. Overhead
    a chopper, cropping our last contrition

    as easily as a boy with a stick
dispatches thistle-heads, riots a slow, roaring
    descent to the embassy roof:
and one arrival rifles our silence of love,
    of the truths we had been shoring
    against our future. Now we are all sick.

    We are leaving, leaving. Impolitic
to stay. Imprudent. Impossible. And the men
    who biked the long hot dusty roads
to bring us the news, and carried our chosen loads
    out of the last hotels, have gone,
    knowing we're going. Now we are all sick.

    We are sick in strange ways, and with a pain
we thought belonged in other lives; and we climb high
    from the scene of our crimes, needing
escape from the heat, the helplessness, the bleeding,
    battering to an angry sky
    where thunder breeds, bringing releasing rain.

Brunei

Down Jalan Sultan the Datsuns burn,
exulting, declaiming:
we shall inherit the earth.

Querulous, squalling, squealing like kids at the dodgems:
the neurasthenic staccatissimo
Of acquisition in action.

When we arrived, and entered the port, and anchored,
the holy body of brightness, the beautiful fire,
burned like the tongues of deity high in the dark.

Stitching in and out the spindle stilts,
Suzuki outboard motors split
the water village stillness, taking

Moslem girls in white and blue to school.
Women are hanging the washing out,
and up the rickety walkway races

Brunei's young executive,
pin-striped trousers, attaché case, and late,
making the frail stilettos creak and sway.

The morning of the following day, the ninth of July,
the king of the island sent a magnificent prau
with workings in gold at bow and stern

and banners of blue and white and peacock feathers.
Their chiefs presented us with a painted jar
filled with betel and areca, a fruit,

two cages full of fowls, and sugarcane, and goats,
and jars of spirit, called arak. The spirit of these people
is clear as water, and very strong.

The hovels are balanced on their stalks
precarious as dandelion clocks.
The river slubbers, lapping at

the slobby mudflats, slopping at
rotting rats and bottles, bamboo poles,
cans and tyres and crappy scum.

The river drivels dirty yellow.
The swimming children love it.
We were taken on elephant-back to visit the king,

and seven bearers went ahead with gifts:
velvet robes and velvet-covered chairs,
a gilded writing-case, and silvered shoes.

The king of Spain, their king declared,
shall be my friend.
Three hundred naked guards with rapiers

smiled with a single smile
that slit along the sides of the great hall
like a slash from a blade.

Evening at Imogiri

The bullock carts are pulling back along
the homeward road, below the hillside where
the spirits of the Javan kings confer
knowledge of heaven on the empty air.

The cool of evening light, the cool of time
received and seen: the meanings of the day
fading, changing. Cold perceptions of night
a single cigarette away.

At kitchens by the wayside women sit,
shrivelled into a silence and a mask,
like matchlit faces in a cinema.
And frangipani falling in the dusk.

Mother of Battles

I

Lady of the cypress and the cedar
Lady of the land between the rivers
Lady of the silence of the stones
the dusty silence in the olive grove
the dusty silence in the vineyard he
was toiling all the morning all
the afternoon at night he said
you looked like Madonna like Marilyn
Monroe like Greta Garbo like Jean
Harlow he said that your breasts
were like clusters of dates like
clusters of grapes on the vine
like clusters of dumb iron bombs
the voice of the B52 is heard in the land

II

Lady of the land between the rivers
Lady of Uruk and Babylon
the souks the avenues the alleyways
the secret places of the stairs the
clefts of the rock the shelters underground
the dusty silence in the olive grove
the dusty silence in the vineyard he
was toiling all the morning all
the afternoon at night he said
it's like a fuck you've got to get
the moment right my country 'tis
of thee and then you bomb the shit out

[18]

III

Lady of the warring and the loving
Lady of the waters and the earth
Lady of the Stratofortresses
unloading over Nasiriyeh he
knew all the secret places knew the cleft
the centrefold the UN resolution
he said that it felt like the fit of a stone
in a peach he said that your pussy'd
got to be the plummiest pot
he'd ever packed his payload in
we ve got to get that fucking asshole
over on your belly Lady
hey Saddam the 52nd
coming coming up
soddom soddom

IV

Lady of mallows and tangled anise
Lady of the dusty silences
the olive grove the river and the vineyard
he tucked your scented knickers in his helmet
the perfume of your favour gave him head
he hardened to the killing Lady
all the morning all the afternoon oh
Lady of the garden and at
night he said I wish that I was dead
I wish that I was with the men
who lie in zippered plastic sheaths
and slide into a sleep they never wake from

2 The Gas Mask Dance

I

Garcia said he carries cards
black cards death cards
aces of spades I said
why five of them not fifty
Garcia said the way he figured it
the odds were that he'd be
the sixth in line to die
he's pissed that they won't let him wear
his Rambo Rag he left his sperm
on ice in San Diego
                              so
I'm sitting in the sun
cleaning my M-16 and
feeling immortal and
singing along with the
walkman wonderful
counsellor and I'm
far from the Kuwaiti
theatre I'm in another
life and I'm under the table
with Salvador and I'm kissing
his eatable meat sweet Jesus
let me survive let me
go home alive and be
thrown out again of Tocqueville's
Bistro back in Dayton
                              oh I
want to know the flesh
the body and the blood

I want my own messiah and
his name shall not be callèd
Norman Schwarzkopf
                    over there
that guy's Brinkofski
wearing mafioso shades and
shlepping his M-60 and
his sousaphone and looking
supercool I love him don't
you love him too

        II

Over and over I'm telling myself
I'm immortal immortal
I always remember
the herdsman I saw in
the sandstorm that morning
protectively tucking
a goat in the folds
of his stoical cloak
we drove to the camp
and there were Garcia
and Eddie Dumuzi
doing the Gas Mask Dance
jiving all angles as if
their strings were cut but
still twitching alive
                    so
call me immortal in the sun
the goddess of the M-16
you got to keep your weapon clean
and still I'm singing out
despisèd rejected

Garcia Dumuzi
I love you
        Dumuzi's
collecting statistics
he told me that Schwarzkopf
wakes fifteen or twenty
times nightly to worry
I said tell me Eddie you're
saying there's times when he sleeps

        III

Call me immortal
my body is stoppered
I'm snug in a body
boots and battledress
got my belt and knife
my M-16 my walkman
I'm alive
        and I shall go
to the pit
        to the palace
of lapis lazuli

3 THE DESCENT

I

She went to the palace of lapis lazuli
the pit the great below the underworld

at the first door
he took the headset from her head
unclipped the walkman from her belt

why have you taken my walkman away
a woman needs her music needs
the rhythms of the body needs the
rhythms of the spirit

                    quiet Inanna
this is the law of the underworld
the law must be obeyed

II

She went to the palace of lapis lazuli
the pit the great below the underworld

at the second door
he took the M-16 from her hand
removed the magazine

why have you taken my M-16 away
didn't they tell you anything a
woman needs her weapon wants to feel
she can defend herself

                    quiet Inanna
this is the law of the underworld
the law must be obeyed

III

She went to the palace of lapis lazuli
the pit the great below the underworld

at the third door
he took the knife that slept at her side
unclasped the belt about her waist

why have you taken my knife and belt away
haven't you ever heard that a woman
has to challenge and subvert the
code of the male

        quiet Inanna
this is the law of the underworld
the law must be obeyed

IV

She went to the palace of lapis lazuli
the pit the great below the underworld

at the fourth door
he took the heavy duty boots
laced high above her ankles

why have you taken my boots away
men are always the same they want to
prevent you from walking so they can say
what pretty feet you've got

        quiet Inanna
this is the law of the underworld
the law must be obeyed

V

She went to the palace of lapis lazoli
the pit the great below the underworld

at the fifth door
he took the desert battledress
that camouflaged her flesh

why have you taken my battledress away
men are always the same they only
want you in your lingerie then
preferably out of it

                quiet Inanna
this is the law of the underworld
the law must be obeyed

VI

She went to the palace of lapis lazuli
the pit the great below the underworld

at the sixth door
he took the Italian bodystocking
stripped the body from her body

why have you taken my body away
I want you to know that I wear black lace
to please myself and myself alone I
hope you're satisfied

                quiet Inanna
this is the law of the underworld
the law must be obeyed

VII

She went to the palace of lapis lazuli
the pit the great below the underworld

at the seventh door
he took the string between her thighs
and pulled the stopper of her blood

why have you taken my Mary away
this is my body this is my blood
I'm naked and defenceless this
is a woman

      quiet Inanna
this is the law of the underworld
the law must be obeyed

4 REDEMPTION

I

They said that I had gassed the Kurds
Jews gypsies homosexuals soldiers
in Abyssinia and at Ypres
I said that I was naked and defenceless

They said that I had napalmed Vietnam
bombed Dresden and Hiroshima
and killed the innocents on Nasir bridge
I said that I was naked and defenceless

They said that I was at the Winter Palace
Amritsar Lidice I slaughtered
Incas blacks and aborigines
I said that I was naked and defenceless

They said that I ran Auschwitz and the Gulag
I was the hemlock Socrates had drunk
the vinegar a soldier offered Christ
I said that I was naked and defenceless

II

In the pit my judges cast me down
accused me cursed me called me
Lady of the F-16s and MiGs
the Patriots the Scuds they spat
in my face they smeared my breasts with shit
they took a razor to my labia
they said that I would do the same to them
and then they said that I was free to leave

on one condition
              only if I sent
the one who was my cypress and my cedar
my lily and my thorn my love and war
to take my place in the pit

          III

I thought of Saddam
his 16-metre arms
cast in Basingstoke
by Tallix Morris Singer
metal melted down
from dead Iraqi guns
uplifted carrying
the sword of Qadisiyya
round the wreck the lone
and level sands
stretch far away
                    I
thought of Stormin' Norman
lover of the opera and
ballet amateur
magician fluent in
German and French and
humanely concerned
about casualties
his wife back in Tampa
Florida worrying
whether Norman's
eating right
              I thought
of Garcia with his aces
and his sperm on ice
Brinkofski with his shades
and shiny sousaphone
or Eddie Dumuzi

doing the Dance with the
tail of a rattler he
killed at Fort Worth in his
pocket for luck
                    then
I thought of my Salvador
flesh of my flesh
blood of my blood
mortal lover
walker on my
water
        till at last
I remembered the herdsman
I saw in the sandstorm
that morning protectively
tucking a goat in the
folds of his cloak
                    and I knew

5 LAMENT FOR THE HERDSMAN

Changed he is changed he
is dusted with silence

my heart is birdsong in a wilderness

                    9–11 FEBRUARY 1991

[29]

Homo Sum

a response to Günter Kunert

One day, friend, we will all be statistics too.
    Not much comfort in that, I admit.
But think of the bureaucrat busy with records of *you*,
    filing the facts: the consistency of your shit,
the length of your hair, the cleanliness of your collars,
    your liking for Dizzy Gillespie, George Herbert and pasta,
your monthly purchasing power (computed in dollars).
    How, in this age, is the jerk to know man from master?

True, the masters will write the history books.
    They'll call it an egalitarian age.
Everyone had a fair share of the money and women and looks.
    That's what they'll say. In black and white. Page after page
                                                after page.
True. But still no one has ever forgotten the cry
    that struck the noise of the history lecturers dumb,
the cry of the slaves and the masters alike of a civilization about
                                                to die:

    homo sum.

What if our cry survives?
    Would that not be liberty: setting a precedent
for other times and other lives?
    Is memory not its own monument?
Friend, it seems we do nothing but talk of our graves.
    As if we possessed it already, we talk of the earth.
Me, I'll not lie with the owners. Truly, I'll lie with the slaves.
    Our mouths, one and all, will be stopped with liberty's dirt.

That Christmas

We were joking with Prussians
and Württembergers
we could have slaughtered
only hours before,
offering cigarettes
and showing photographs
and singing 'Auld Lang Syne',

when up jumped a plump
and puzzled hare
from the cabbage patch
and Captain Hulse called out
holloa and one and all
we followed the animal over
the frozen earth and killed it.

Heathrow

This might be the kind of place you'd pause for a while,
    as Auden visited the grave of Freud
    or Larkin on his bike stopped at a church,
        a place to chill the head

with transit, fraughtness, fear, the ache of departure –
    keeping one eye on the board and one on
    the bag you mustn't leave unattended.
        Whatever you thought you

believed translates as a traffic in hope. Chanel.
    Gucci leather. Hermès silk. Gordon's gin. Love.
    From here you can go anywhere. Because.
        Because you can. Because

the commerce of futures and regeneration
    demands your flight. Because there's a census
    that summons you home to your native parts.
        Home to be crucified.

All checked in and nowhere to go. The whole wide world
    is yours, a world well serviced, brightly lit.
    No place on earth would sooner start a prayer.
        When body bags are flown

back home from the war zones where once you vacationed,
    Big Brother's dogs will sniff out the arseholes
    of corpses for illegal substances.
        When the conspirators

dangle on the piano wire, they'll twitch their last
    in hangars that house the Boeings that bear
    economy and first to higher life.
        And when the bloody Guard

have butchered the emperor they've declared insane
    they'll march with his head on a lance and put
    the empire up for auction at Harry
        Ramsden's, Terminal 1,

where, spreading his hands to a global dominion
    of mushy peas, brown sauce and vinegar,
    great Harry, in a photo on the wall,
        grins broadly in July

of 1952, when fish and chips still cost
    three ha'pence, and anyone could tell you
    it didn't taste right unless you ate it
        out of a newspaper.

Nine Points of the Nation

I

Living on this island in the
    American sphere of influence, where
the crappy drollery of history
    crackles across the daily air
reminding us that boredom is
    banal and for ridiculous reasons
will re-elect the ill-intentioned,
    you'll learn a yearning for exile.

II

After they sealed
    the airfield off
with seven miles
    of razor wire,
they counted the cost:
    the several millions
of pounds, the pulse
    beat of fear.

III

The head of our government likes
    to be photographed with children.

IV

Syntax gone rigid in the mouth.
    A seven-year-old hanged at Norwich
for stealing a petticoat. Crows crying *dirt*!
    Your work will set you free.

V

Beautiful Old York paving stones,
    rectangular, in good
condition, ex-public footpath.
    Offered at £80 per ton
plus VAT including carriage.
    Free genuine Victorian street lamp
complete, worth £300,
    with every order of 16 tons or more.

VI

Pepys came on Lady Sandwich "doing
    something upon the pot" in the dining-room.

VII

Here at Tyburn Tree we sit
    in Mother Proctor's Pews.
The nation's full of public shit.
    This is the six o'clock news.

VIII

I've never liked this city, not
    compared with Vienna, say, or Amsterdam.
It has a small and smutty atmosphere,
    the cramped crush of a city that has got
and spent: a truthless tract written
    in stale legitimation of Britain.
I visit and choke on the pride.
    That mighty heart is lying, still!

IX

Come out from the dark, my love, we'll ride to where
    the Underground comes up for light and air.

1985

Dole Queue

Tom Paine at one time made
ladies' corsets. And why not? I too had
a job once, I remember, on
an assembly line.

Seems a long time ago.
Every fucking Monday I stand here, grow
grey-faced, slack; I slouch. What do I
care about the law,

ain't I got the power? said
Cornelius Vanderbilt. Went to bed
last night, the wife says, common sense
doesn't stand a chance

when you're up against profit,
I says to her, you don't want to say that
too loud, can we have the light off
now? It's a rip-off,

she says, the whole caper.
See what it said today in the paper?
Go to sleep, Glad, I says. Tom Paine,
refused a seat on

the stagecoach, was told by
the passengers to fear the Lord's wrath. I
wonder at times what has become
of justice if some

can buy their own. I won't
pretend to understand the world. I don't.
One night we sat and watched the stars,
listened to the cars

on the carriageway back
of our house. The stars were bright, the night black.
Why, says Glad, are we landed with
a life before death?

The Bell-ringer

after Vladimir Bukovsky

    When it started
that first morning it was pleasant
when the meadows were wet and the
        mist hung low on the fields
                to hear

        the stirring of
compassionate hearts moved by the
bells. The strength of the pull grew through
        the people's sinews: they
                knew why

        they believed, that
morning. At midday, when the smell
of pies and rye-cakes settled with
    ·   the bells in alleys, they
                began

        to be puzzled,
yes: but no one had died, no one
been born; so they ate well, and thought
        no more about it. When
                that dull

        sleepy-eyed end
of afternoon arrived, the shower
of sound continuing from the
        tower, melancholy set
                in, and

          some of them thought
of their dead and wept. At sunset
down by the water it was so
        beautiful: melodic,
                measured,

          everything in
harmony. You know what I mean.
But that night suddenly it was
        no longer a joke, no
                one slept,

          there was a strange
fear abroad, barring shutters and
shooting bolts.
                        And so it went on
        for several days and
                nights. You

          can't imagine
the tension, the madness: people
dancing, not walking, and praying
        aloud in the market
                place, and

          weeping, getting
on each other's nerves, the old men
sick, the young men wild, the women
        fasting, frantic for their
                last days.

On the fifth day
the pealing stopped. Weak and staggered
by silence, they went up into
    the belfry, and found him
        there, and

    unclenched his hands
from the cold ropes. His face was black,
his lips were bloodied. Not that there
    was any life left in
        his time.

Fornicating and Reading the Papers

I

John Stubbs of Lincoln's Inn has written a pamphlet:
The Discoverie of a Gaping Gulf
to swallow England by a French Marriage.
The queen has seen the pamphlet, at least
the title page. She is burning with choler.
She says this Stubbs is a seditious villain.

This is the stage set up in the market place
at Westminster. This is seditious Stubbs.
This is the butcher's knife, keen against his wrist.
This is the mallet that strikes against the knife.
The moment his right hand is off, seditious Stubbs
doffs his hat with his left, crying *God save the queen*!

II

Wet from the shower
towelling your breasts
you ask me if I've read
Motley's *Rise of the Dutch Republic.*

My heart is in another question: *What*
is the price of a virtuous woman?
Ads in the London Underground reply:
Buy her a diamond before someone else does.

III

The Sudanese minister shrugs. *It is only a hand,*
    he declares, *a small price to pay*
for the preservation of law and order.
    The minister drums his fingers on the desk.

This is the guilty man, whose hand
    was found in another man's pocket.
He watches the amputation carefully.
    No noble words are waiting in his mouth,
no thoughts of God or saving in his head.

    His hand is preserved in a jar of surgical alcohol.

IV

A dusty lane
    in the polder
the flat
    loveliness
and the high
    cloud-shattered sky
caressed by alders
    the room where we lay
shuttered against the day
    breathing
the white smell
    of apples in the loft
the fragrance of grass
    the touch of it:
for days I was whistling
    those bars from the rondo
movement of Beethoven's first
    piano concerto.

V

He is a missionary. From Detroit.
    They, the Sendero Luminoso, know
that he is the CIA. America made flesh.
    Into that flesh they drive needles, beneath
the toenails. One of his eyes has been pulped
    by a rifle-butt. They have crushed his testicles.

They know what they know. They are the gods
    on the shining path of righteousness.
Now they hack off his fingers one by one.
    Unable to give the answers they require,
My God, why hast thou he breathes, and
    passes out again, till the pain revives him.

VI

María said to Yerma
    Haven't you held
a living bird in your hand?
    well that's what it's like,
having a child inside,
    only more in the blood.

Burslem

It is very well to say: Plutarch and Alfieri loved Chæronea and Asti.
Loved them and left them. In this fashion I also will love my native place
when far from it.
Leopardi

For ages I thought that the famous comedian
      Arthur Askey lived in Burslem,
   quishing and quishing his glittering knives
in a reek that was seawater, sawdust and death,

and filleting, grinning and chuckling, a glint in his
      glasses, selling us plaice, chinkling
   George Rex, Elizabeth Reg, the shillings
and pence in his striped apron pocket, and wiping

and wringing his hands: *Thank you, thanking you kindly.* The
      sign on the shop read *A. Askey:*
   Fish, Game and Poultry. Halibut bedded
on ice amid plastic tomatoes and parsley.

Button-eyed pheasants. Rabbits drip-drippeting crimson.
      Askey pushing his mongering
   boater up off his forehead to listen
to pips and a Home Service voice. Are these thoughts home?

What is the point of remembering Cox's entry?
      They're boarded over now, the thick
   black glossy timbers; gone, the fat number
bossed in gold above the door; the painted plaster

girl who stood in the chemist's doorway, holding a box
      marked Spastics, is gone, and gone is
   the chemist's as well, where they sold the sticks
of barley sugar I'd suck oh so slowly till

all that was left was a golden glow. Was sweetness. Light.
        Whose life was that? What child was that?
    What am I hurting for?
                            Much of my life
I despised and detested the place I was born.

I hadn't a good word to say about Stoke on Trent,
        its philistine dreariness, lack
    of a spirit, of anything better
than getting and spending, money and muck. But now

I often catch myself wondering what it was like
        when Wedgwood called his factory
    Etruria. The gentle land. A breath
of elder and briar and grasses on the air.

I think of Arnold Bennett looking down to Burslem
        only a century ago:
    the curving earthy road ran down the hill
between the leafy green to where the brick-built town

nestled among the hills in a pall of smoke, almost
        as picturesque as Flemish towns.
    When I was a boy, the buckets of slag
whined overhead at Smallthorne colliery. Grime

fell from the air. The backstreets off Hamil Road where Dad
        grew up were the prowling grounds of
    youths who punched me and stole from me. Grim. And
unbeautiful. Unoriginal. What can it

mean, to say I miss the bleared Burslem I grew up with?
        I wouldn't want to live there now.
    But still: it seems so human and so rich,
to start with high ideals among these English hills

and end so appallingly soon in this dereliction,
      where it's a comfort knowing once
    the sisters, Constance and Sophia Baines,
pressed up their noses at that window. That one. There.

After Rain

Clouds at the edge: but there, above
    a thin stretch, a slim arc
    of light. The sky's alive
with dull movement; the moon consumes the dark
like Ugolino gnawing at the skull
    of Ruggieri. Full

    circle, now: white, bright. And some force
    pushes you out into
    the garden, to the source
of that strange fragrance: sage, earth and mint. You
dug up those chives when the wind blew you down
    that steep hill to Walltown,

    where some Spaniard with a fine tongue,
    serving with the legion
    at the Wall, had begun
his own herb garden, brought to a region
of gales and blizzards Spanish sun. Unless
    the heart's hard arbitress

    releases you, you will be caught
    forever in this sphere
    of self-inceptive thought,
the metamorphosis of year to year,
and each remembered moonlit night will be
    scented with sanctity.

Europe

1

Somewhere in this European darkness
a woman is waiting at a window,
watching the falling snow.

Somewhere in this European darkness
a man is leading a child home. Both are
tired now, but it's not far.

Somehow in this solitary darkness
we find our way to the station and stand
silently hand in hand.

Meetings and departures: the map, networked
with track, shows us the routes that take us back
to origins we lack.

What shall we say were the reasons we passed
our chances by tonight? For we have passed
our chances by. Our last.

2

Today we have been out in the fields,
drawing conclusions from blades of grass.

We have learnt: after rain the earth stirs.
We have learnt: there is warmth at the world's

core. We have identified soldiers
known and unknown, murdered and missing,

posted outside Derry pubs or on
East European borders, sitting

in bars in Nuremberg, lounging in
restaurants overlooking the Rhine.

We have seen the sun set in the sea
where we presume the States to be, seen

it rise again over the Georgian
Republic. In silent cathedrals

we have watched the candles burning low
till an altar boy comes and snuffs them.

3

The woman at the window, withdrawing,
letting the curtain fall, repossessing
herself in an empty room, and crossing
herself as she crosses the room:

children chasing shadows in the garden,
acting out the deaths of the fathers of
children who play the same games in countries
whose names they have read on maps:

under a scattered dazzle of starlight,
grey and waking, the soldier, staring out
at the night, wondering why, by what right
it now stares back with such hostility:

too much there is that can be made a word
and spoken in a dark doorway at night,
mouth to mouth like a kiss: ah why were we
born to be in this place at this time?

1977

II Burnings

Twentieth Burning in the Bishopric of Wurzburg

Today we rose early. The autumn smells
of wet air and fallen leafage and rotting
apples and plums and pears were crisped by frost
at that hour. The mist, settled on the hills,
did not, I noticed, lift until midday.

Today we did good work and burnt six. One
was Goebel's girl, Anna, for many here
in Wurzburg the city's greatest beauty;
sixteen and, it is true, with a certain
freshness; but we cannot make exceptions.

Another, and one whom, I must confess,
I secretly regret, was young Bernhard,
who played the oboe on April evenings
in his room overlooking the deacon's
garden. He spoke several languages.

Then the two boys, the twins, the butcher's boys,
twelve years of age, both of them brats. One day
I watched Alfred, the younger, I believe,
by twenty minutes, crush a starling's head.
The bird was helpless, had broken a wing.

And there was Stepper's daughter, Suzannah,
a six-year-old, but already able
to help her father considerably,
who, let's face it, is a foolish cripple,
and easily the city's worst cobbler.

Last on the list for today, the creature
who kept the bridge gate: I don't even know
her name, but remember that as she passed
her odour nearly knocked me out. No loss
to anyone, filthy old so-and-so.

I noticed Frau Braunach among the crowd.
She's looking older. We burnt her husband,
the senator, the lecherous old lump,
a year or so ago. Funny how it
attracts above all those who have lost most.

It went off very quietly; we sang
till the flames were quite low. Weydenbusch, who
succeeded Schwerdt as choir-master, tells me
this year's will be an excellent vintage.
And he should know, he owns half the vineyards
round the town. I must see to the cellars.

A Family Portrait circa 1900

Going blackly back to the old unknown
looking like this! Father, frowning
the future out of countenance;

his beautiful wife wearing a greedy smile
that is smugly defiant, as if she had been caught
secretly nursing proprietary guilt.

Can she suppose nobody knows?
Her eyes are ablaze with praise to the Lord
the Almighty; but she looks bored.

She rests a white hand on the cold shoulder
of the unconsoled girl sitting in front.
Her daughter. Hers for life.

The Prisoner

after Rilke

Suppose that what to you is wind and sky,
air that you breathe
and brightness to your eye,

abruptly turns to hurt,
all but that proper part
where your hands are, and your heart;

and what is *tomorrow* to you now,
or *later, then, next year, forever,*
the future sense of promises and hope,

becomes a present tense of pain,
a festering impurity
filling up with suffering;

everything that was you
is nothing but a rawness and a wrong;
and he who once you thought was God

is your gaoler, spiteful, pausing outside
your cell to give you filthy looks.
And still you live.

Phrenology, 1914

The music room is cool and blue.
The Essen engineer, her father's friend,
holds the white china head in his broad hands

and examines the cold bald spaces which
a Staffordshire manufacturer has inscribed:
sublimity, benevolence, philoprogenitiveness.

Fräulein Evi finishes, and lays the flute aside.
Bumps on the head, he informs her, smiling,
were said to indicate the size of the brain.

Amazing what people will believe.
Again the supercilious smile
of a man who is on smiling terms with the future.

She knows he has travelled: Morocco, Mexico . . .
She knows the clubmen call him a man of the world.
Her father supposes she will learn to like him.

She knows he holds her father in contempt
for his beliefs, for unfastening his braces after dinner,
for smoking a strong Havana with his cognac.

I think there is a crack across my skull.
He joins her at the window. *It*
will open wide if he touches me.

Magnolia's candescent pallor
cups to candle-flames in the deep green:
waxy ephemera, epigrams of the spirit.

I love you, Evi. And
from far in villa gardens where
the Wannsee air stirs the stillness

and all the August afternoon
innumerable murmurings of bees
negotiate their treaties in the shade

of heavy scented lindens,
an empire's dead imperatives
command immediate consent.

I walked in a poppy field at Potsdam.
Flags of scarlet hanging loose
like rags of slashed flesh.

I put my lips to the petals
and kissed the taste of forgetting.
Who can know what is happening in my head?

When they said we were at war
my mouth went dry with the bleached
taste of the host, like a wafer of wax.

But he is too old to fight and be killed.
I think it may be good to love the dead.
I think I shall scream if he touches me again.

Striking his thigh with a silver-headed cane,
her father crosses the lawn, smiling
to see the engineer stroking her hair.

He is explaining to Reinwald the lawyer
that this our city, our Berlin,
is the nerve centre of the Reich:

all of us must do what we know to be right,
for here we are most sensitive to hurt.
Once more and I shall scream. I wish I could die.

One day I walked out on the Wannsee shore
where Henriette Vogel went with Kleist.
After he had shot her through the heart

he shot himself in the mouth with a second pistol,
and suffocated on the choking smoke
of the powder. Their smiles are smothering me.

White

Josef Gebhard, 1895–1967

Contentment dwelt under the pear tree where
he'd sit in the shade on a kitchen chair
    in shirtsleeves and braces,
his back to the beans and the dahlias,

hands like motoring gloves on his breast,
a cotton handkerchief draped on his face
    to show he was resting.
His handkerchiefs were a faded white, like

old snow or sloeflower, smelling of snowmelt,
of maleness and trouser pocket. He'd sit
    in the garden, listen
to chickens, bees, a neighbour's radio,

and close his eyes. And be in Astrakhan.
The prison camp. The hospital. The sky
    as bold and white as an
enamel bowl. As functional and bare.

I remember one day in the forest
we stopped at an anthill. *Don't poke at it*
    he told me quietly.
We stood there in the resin-scented shade,

watching the ants in the pine-needle hill
built high as my chest, working, unresting.
    He took the handkerchief
from his pocket, flapped it open, and placed

it carefully on the hill. *Now watch*. I watched.
He waited till the cloth was black with ants,
    then shook it clear. *Now put
your nose to it*. And instantly my head

filled with the formic acid reek of fear,
the thing he wanted me to understand:
      a white-out in the mind,
white as the heavens over Astrakhan,

white as the cool of an afternoon hour
in a sunshot garden under a pear
      tree, all of contentment
dwelling in the tent of a square of cloth.

Refugees

All night I've been driving this hearse of sleep
through dreams of dying, stunned by the dark,
and waking to the morning feel I've walked
into a photograph of war:
                                        across
the clods that litter a ploughed and stubborn field
three women come stumbling towards me,
a stooped old baggage in black and her daughters
struggling under the weight of refugee luggage,
picking an improvised footing through the furrows.
They're carrying too much. Their load's too cumbersome.
Sooner or later they'll have to leave something behind.
I watch them toil with their cases and basket,
negotiating a passage across the day
where minute after remembering minute
burns away like the farmhouse at their backs,
the smoke of the bombed-out past staining
the grey indifference of the heavens.
                                                        Will
they walk right past? Without a word to me?
Where will they go? And will there be a season
when someone sees the seed green in the field?

On Location

for Peter and Odile Wagner

This superannuated Bavarian town
    of crumbling baroque and flaking façades
is the perfect backdrop for these shameful charades.
    It is a dull place which neither renown
nor notoriety has ever disgraced, so
    it is only fitting that this film crew
should choose to engender their legend of a Jew,
    his Aryan wife, and the Gestapo
here on this unhistoric square (for, after all,
    the innocent present is the fittest
set on which to play actions of the guilty past,
    since there we see the full ironical
force of historical fact). Thus the director
    sits in his canvas chair smoking cigars,
snapping Hollywood commandments at timid stars,
    his belly in his lap, his green visor
pushed back into his straight black hair. Incessantly
    the make-up girl paints, the clapperboard snaps,
and cameras capture the frail, final (perhaps)
    fitness of inevitability,
filming reality into fiction, fiction
    into reality: who can tell which?
With luck this movie will make its producer rich,
    will even be seen on television
in Israel and the States, Japan and Germany.
    Tourists who visit this town in future
will tell each other that was Aaron's house, and there
    was where he said goodbye to Rosemary.

One Damn Thing after another

The elementary logic of farewells
is a bore, you say, belittling yourself and over-
eager to confess to a hatred of tears. Your

father was found at the wheel of his taxi
this morning at three. The engine was ticking
over, the headlights were on. You describe how

you watched the rainwater filling into the
lilac, how the police light flashing
off the cobbles made you dizzy. Goodbye.

A nineteen-year-old GI. He'd thrown the
knife into the grass. His denim jacket
was in the back of the taxi, with his ID.

Aschaffenburg, you always used to say,
was a quiet town where nothing ever happened.
So mathematical! A castle

with twelve towers and fifty-two doors
and three hundred and sixty-five windows.
I've never checked it myself. But I take your point:

after a night like this you'll learn to hate
the cool exactness of sunlight calling forth
the daily confident enlightenment.

Your mother sent him a letter when
they were still engaged, breaking it off,
but somehow the letter fetched up in a sack

of mail for Asia, and sat in a boat
in the Suez Canal for years, really, for years,
till they opened it up again. By then

your parents had long been married, and you were eight
and learning the violin, and one day, a Tuesday,
the letter arrived, and your father never

felt safe in his love again. Imagine it: how
the daily hello of living disintegrates.
Goodbye goodbye goodbye goodbye goodbye.

I have a plane to make, but I'll listen
here on the windy platform, till my train comes in;
you'll tell me whatever histories you will,

until the hysteria gets the better of you. I
will write you a letter from the departure lounge
in Frankfurt. You ought to be with your mother.

Festival of Youth

East Berlin

The Stasis lean on their armoured cars,
smoking. Alert.
Attendance is by invitation only.

After the rally the Freie Deutsche Jugend
gulp apple juice in paper cups.
The stretcher-bearers relax.

One fourteen-year-old blueshirt wants to be
a frontier guard.
Responsible, rewarding and important.

The problem with schoolkids, he complains,
is generating motivation.
All this lot want is rock and roll and hockey.

1979

To Botho Strauss in Berlin

Your cool high-ceilinged life
is naked as a stage,

as if you'd taken an apartment where
the set-designer of your dreams

had recently moved out.
It is a theatre after the première,

filled up to emptiness with applause.
I think of God the Almighty after the ball,

sitting as you imagined him
on the palace steps, asleep in his slippers and topper.

Let there (he mumbles in his slumber,
dreamy and calmly afraid) *be light.*

Roadworkers Picking Cherries

The first, wearing rumpled cords belted with clothes-line,
    climbs on the wall where the shade crumples and
flaps, and takes off the hat that reminds him of the
    wine he drank sitting under a fig tree
in a Sicilian village. The straw is frayed
    and feathering at the crown, but he holds
the hat in a pinch of affection, the fonder
    of it the more it weathers, and fans the
air to cool his face. From the fields the laughter of
    children. The fragrance of hay. He reaches
up to the dark blood-coloured cherries and plucks and
    drops a fruit in his hat, then another,
and goes on picking, contented, feeling the warmth
    of the afternoon. It is good. His hat
is filling.
        The younger man in blue overalls
    is thinking how peaceful the silence is
now they've switched off the generator.
                Soon there are
    five of them up on the wall, picking and
laughing and spitting the stones in the orchard grass,
    and the man with the hat has eaten through
to the base of the crown, which is stained with juice, and
    he sits at the dusty roadside, and pulls
the brim of his hat to shadow his brow, hearing
    the single excitement of a lark and
knowing the dark red stains in his hat will forever
    recall a day when he sat with the taste
of cherries in his mouth and looked out on the fields
    fading to pale blue in the distant hills.

Loreley

for Michael Claridge

Ich weiß nicht, was soll es bedeuten,
daß ich so traurig bin . . . though who could sit
by the cold river, watching the lights

of the opposite bank, St Goarshausen,
shake in the ferry's wake, then settle again
to a steady glow of gold

molten on the flow (und ruhig
fließt der Rhein), and not
know that this is the off-season

of love . . .? Ein Märchen aus alten Zeiten,
das kommt mir nicht aus dem Sinn: in
the corner the cook is drinking himself silly,

telling the boss and the barman for
the third time this evening the story about
the Danzig whore. Presently they sing.

They seem to have made no preparations for winter,
but nothing will stop their noise, not even the silence,
not even the autumn's big and childless voids.

To Gottlob Fabian

died at Tarnast, 4 March 1844

In Vormärz Brandenburg
six iron generations back
across the blood and soil
you worked a windmill at Tarnast.

I know your stolid windmill,
gentle and firm, wooden and white,
set on the flats of Brandenburg,
tenderly taking the wind.

I know the stones, the stones that grind,
the principle of what is fine.
I know your watchfulness, your eye,
your patience, and your sky:

we are sails of the same windmill
stilled, tensed to a nameless, windstill
breathing culled from the very air,
again becoming air.

III Holy Lands

The Winter Ward

Snow the nurse
is turning down
the city sheets
with a hospital frown.

Not far, my love,
not far to go,
only another
block or so.

Night the doctor
is walking the dark
with living daylights
in his heart.

Not far, my love,
to the winter ward,
to the surgeon's knife
in the House of the Lord.

The Country of Pain and Revelation

The woman sitting on the glinting barrier
watching a stir of air relentlessly uplift
    the silver undersides of leaves
  is breathing very carefully, as if

afraid that she might be too tender for breathing.
Her hand is resting in the dusty hair of the
    man lying jack-knifed on the grass
  between the glittering strips of metal

that run down the centre reserve. She does not see
the slowed traffic, the flashing lights approaching. She
    is elsewhere. Again the country
  of pain and revelation has a guest.

Again the great light has ground the peaks to powder.
Again in the valleys the shadows have sheltered
    the traveller standing alert
  at the rail of the ferry, the trader

bargaining with the goatherd, and the trapper, still
and meticulous in his secretive sidelight.
    It is the discovered country
  from which, returning in wonder as if

from memories of the dreams we thought forgotten,
we sunder in awe, wanting. What is the meaning
    of graining in a rockface? What
  annunciation hides in a hut built

high on an outcrop overlooking the nowhere,
bared to the higher nowhere of the air? And why must
    we find that after our truest
  transmigrations, after our fertile hopes,

we still are left with smashed metal and glass, resting
fingers in the hair of a dying lover? She
        knows the name of the place. Leaning
      forward, she kisses the dusty lips and

cradles his head and places her cheek against his,
and he learns to say yes, say yes, and goes home to
        a lighted house, a dazzle of
      horror, security, darkness and love.

Knowing

Knowing is movement, like a fly
    sitting in sunlight and
    fretting its forelegs, like
a pantomime miser rubbing his hands:
a callous confidence of possession
    cold as vivisection

    informs the several motions. Flies,
    however, will spread their
    bladed wings and shed skies
of light from off steel-plated gossamer,
shake rainbows, poking blackened cast-iron rods
    like pistons. Only gods

    perform so perfectly. Brilliance,
    though incidental as
    a fly's spectrum abglanz,
is natural. We don't see it, nor is
it given to us to mirror by deception
    light's bright intellection.

Five Poems after Winslow Homer

for Christopher Koch

I   LONG BRANCH, NEW JERSEY
    1869

A northern reconstructionist parade
of confidence and crinolines! as if
    a midday promenade
    on the crest of a sunlit cliff

were equal to the knowledge that dispels
our doubts of an experience of grace:
    the shopgirls and the belles,
    in cotton and velvet and lace,

pursuing their quest for first causes, stop
before oblivion's pavilion
    to review from the top
    the proven conclusions of sun –

each one of them a fresh hypothesis
of flesh, bundled and tucked into bustles
    and berthas. Their hair is
    bobbed and they carry parasols;

see, here are love and vanity and grief,
attested in the rhetoric of light,
    a statement of belief
    said like a charm against the night.

II A BASKET OF CLAMS
1873

Me and my cousin Toby
are walking across the sands
one hand each on the handle
of a basket full of clams.

We've rolled our pants up to the knee
my cousin Toby and me
cos we've been down to fetch the clams
from down at the sea.

There's boats here high up in the dry
and dead fish on the beach
my house is just a short way back
out of the ocean's reach.

My pa says God's in everything
he says we're grains of sand
tickling sharp between God's toes
or held in God's great hand.

My pa says God's in the biggest whale
and the smallest fish that swam
He's in a dogfish and a cod
and even in a clam.

So me and my cousin Toby
are walking across the sands
one hand each on the handle
of a basket full of clams.

III HUNTER IN THE ADIRONDACKS
1892

Because
    and only because
I know
    the way I mean to go, I'll pause
here in the forest underglow
    and listening and looking stand
gun in hand
    at one with the natural laws
I understand.

    What is a man that spends his life in lying?

These are the forests of the Adirondacks:
    the simple imperatives guide my feet
among the praising birches and maples and pines,
    the rusty russets of rotting timbers,
the greens of growing, the golds of dying.
    I know this country like the lines in my hand.
I know the directions, I know the names and numbers.
    I have my trapping wire. My gun. My axe.
I shall survive. I can read the signs.
    I know the self I need to meet.

This is no land
    for theophobiacs.

IV THE FOX HUNT
   1893

Slow
slurred dead-downdragging
faltering floundering step in the deep snow,
strength failing, will flagging,

numbing night
drawing a darkness over the cold white:
a painted fox,
pounding with panic's

pulsebeat bursting in all the important blood,
about to die at the moment of creation.
The fox demands to know the god
of paint and canvas, the god

of the printed page now thirteen lines complete –
but Death is battering
blackly across the immediate
blankness of the moment, the beat of a wing

tears the air with godlike savagery,
impatient of paint. Where is the need
for the fox to die in the snow? we
ask; but berries emblematically bleed,

the crows are cruel, the poem nearly done,
and we know that the real fox, caught
in a greedy creator's grasp, tormented and torn,
will disappear into art, into the death of thought.

V KISSING THE MOON
1904

1

Steadily the salt weed stench,
evil dead sea smell,
fetor of the greedy trench,
deep reek of the swell,

fills the breathing head with fear's
seeping seagreen taint,
reaching past the feral years
from Homer's fathomed paint:

fear breeds, breeds like the ocean's
miseries and joys.
On our terror's tidal motions
ride derisive buoys,

pointing to the hostile rocks
where our hopes went down;
teach me one more paradox,
darling, and I drown.

Teach me Christ is risen for love.
Teach me God is dead.
Teach me of the fiery dove.
Teach me to forget.

2

Onward into night we row,
three men in an Ark:
though the little that we know
brightens the deep dark,

still the light the spirit craves
bides invisible.
At the mercy of the waves,
but closer every pull,

breasting crests of wise desires,
westward we return.
Far to east we see her rise,
cold and kindly moon,

full and virginal and white,
kissed by the fool foam:
we are on a godless tide,
rowing home.

Rotterdam, 07.50, December 22nd

The burners of refineries ignite
    the night:
  the world has lights which the pre-dawn
    conceives in secrecy.
    We've crossed by night, now we
  loll in our compartment, stretch, yawn,

and watch the hunchbacked houses huddled by
    sickly
  orange street lamps, pale in a cold
    mist come off the sea. This
    is Rotterdam CS;
  and from the train we watch the world

melt into morning. Simca, Texaco,
    AGO
  Verzekeringen: human kind's
    identities vanish
    in a grey winter wash.
  Perhaps a painter's job. Not mine.

This is how the shortest day of the year
    starts here:
  with lives seen through picture windows
    like scenes through opened doors
    of advent calendars,
  portraying people no one knows.

At Avila

A poet's distributing photocopied verse
for a few pesetas and a pathetic boy
     tries begging from the woman who
    pulled up in the Porsche in a squall of dust

and now sits testily scanning *La Revista*,
sunglasses cocked in her mane and a pendent breast
     relaxing out of her T-shirt
    whenever she leans for an olive. Me,

I'm watching her over the top of a battered
Penguin Classics *Life of Saint Teresa*, drinking
     an Aguila beer and thinking
    of Teresa's image of the waters –

the difficult and laborious water drawn
from a well, the water moved by a water-wheel,
     the water that flows in a stream,
    and the water that falls from heaven: rain.

The boy's getting nowhere. The woman's ignoring
his mute imploring stare, and she raises her arms
     to stretch, and her flesh lifts as well
    and strains at her shirt, and my denim strains

and pulses for passion in the barren garden.
I return to Teresa's water. What did it
     really mean? That while her spirit
    was busy with God, her body was hot

for a fuck? What of it? I watch as the woman
purses her glistening lips to spit out a pit.
     The boy moves on. To me. I give.
    Graceless and hasty, I give to be rid

of his presence at my pleasures here in the shade
of a cool arcade on the Plaza de Santa
      Teresa. I give, and the boy
   bows with contemptuous gratitude, and

the woman runs a deliberate hand inside
her T-shirt, smiling, like an accomplice in sin.
      If God (wrote Teresa) *withholds*
   the water of grace, no work is enough.

Welcome to the Delectable Mountains

The shadows of our doubts
darken the grass and treetops as we rise.
Here we are at the beginning and end

of all natural scenery, paying our way
up the mountainside: they are taking us
for a ride. The cable car

translates us cautiously to a glacial
pinnacle of inwardness
where Alps on Alps arise

and hang-gliders are stepping off
the cliff-face of Error, purposefully
throwing themselves into nothing.

Look, here you can work a telescope with a coin,
make low the hills and mountains and exalt
the valleys. The closer the landscape comes

the more the grey of distance is upon it:
who will say that seeing is believing?
A girl says it's nothing in summer,

you should be here in the season.
She speaks of snow-capped peaks
and strange exhilarations on the piste,

the singing of air in her ears
and the swift vigour of the down down down
of wishes fulfilled: innocence

perfected in perception of its limits.
She doesn't say quite this;
I am interpreting.

I say it must be quite something,
and she looks at me as if to say
she can see I don't really understand.

In fact I am thinking of a trip
from Hanley High, when I was in the first form:
a fat boy, and the climb up Snowdon was

hot bloody slog, but sliding down the side
could satisfy a boy's imagination.
Excitement and control in one,

sheer energy, the disciplined sense
of descending over the edge of the present tense –
the secret seemed to lie in thinking fast,

thinking past the steps I ought to need:
running down a steep scree,
saving myself with speed.

Horns

Look at Buonarotti's pasta-bearded Moses
slouching like a boxer resting in his corner.

A patriarchal bully-boy.
Mister Universal Law.
With beefy biceps, bodybuilder thighs,
and features modelled on the Pope.
A bruiser of the soul. *With horns.*

Not the fault of Michelangelo.

A mistranslation does the work
of fifty vicars. Exodus
declares that coming down from Sinai
Moses shone. The Vulgate gave him horns.

And every Sunday morning
sexton Jägle crossed the grass
beneath the sycamores
to ask the numbers of the hymns
Herr Schweitzer wanted sung,
and paused to rub a thoughtful thumb
across young Albert's temples, grunting:
Yes, the horns are growing.

The boy heard piping in the forest. And
his cloven-footed fear
went walking on the mountain.

At Aigues-Mortes

*I should like to restore to every subject its weight
and volume, and not only paint the appearance.*
Frédéric Bazille

This is the idea of a day,
this line where land and sky
defy the definition of the eye.

This is the flat
extremity
of extraordinary life:

the levelled end
of the uneven privilege of hills
and the gentle unbending

of rivers and vineyards.
This is elsewhere,
the perfect unending.

Squat-solid at the open-ended scape
the massive majesty of walls,
delineating immanence:

permanence of instinct
properly informing
impermanence of form.

The emblematic act
translates idea
into fact.

Thinking of Bazille, who stood
where I stand now, knowing
that all the strange extremity

of immanence could not atone
for art's apartness, nor restore
propriety to living's dislocations,

I realize we're all the same,
crusading to a holy land
of inviolability.

The Pointlessness of Poetry

for Peter Porter

Small comfort, thinking poetry
the furniture of heart and mind,
if Helen Schlegel's right and only
furniture endures while men and houses perish –

so in the end the world will be
a waste land of poetic chairs and sofas,
desolate through eternity
with not a soul to sit on them.

IV Loves

The Architecture of Air

Though the waters still lap the ghat at Udaipur,
    the Minoan bull still leaps at Knossos,
Frederick's spirit still frets in Knobelsdorff's
    marble halls, and at Azay-le-Rideau
    bankers and kings contest the ghosting rights,

though stupefying superstructures of beauty
    still conform to the paradigms of power,
my lady paints an inch thick, my lord drives a Porsche,
    and fake apartment blocks line the approach
    to Termini when Hitler visits Rome,

our architect is still the architect of air,
    the making mouth, shaping the living breath:
teeth and tongue and lips, building a word or a kiss,
    expressing the inexpressible this.
    Whatever we say is said against death.

The gods are gone: in the Sistine ceiling a crack
    has come between Adam and creation,
the bombs explode in Belfast and Borobudur,
    Petra wears away to ignorant rock.
    Whatever we say is said against death.

Whatever we say is said against death. Adrift,
    listen you whisper, finger to your lips.
The oars shipped, the air unstirring, water dripping
    in stillness. And breathless we wait
    to hear each other say three simple words.

The Kid

Remember seeing him interviewed on TV,
that boy who played opposite Chaplin in *The Kid*?
      Sixty years on, his eyes were dim.
   His meaty carbuncular beet of a nose

was pulsing with veins of imperial purple
that looked like the terrible rubbery bits in
      liver that made your stomach heave
   when you were a kid yourself. Remember? We

tried hard to see the child who had fathered the man,
the scamp in the film, that six-year-old dodger who
      wore his artful innocence tipped
   at a streetwise angle, like his cap. No good:

the child was gone. The boy we'd fallen in love with,
who made us agree we'd like one like him ourselves,
      no longer existed except
   on celluloid. And in our heads. I thought of

that day at the races in Kuching, the little
Filipino girl you couldn't take your eyes off –
      wide-awake, gamine, alive. A
   girl who could be your second self. Or atone

for your abortion? That, I suppose, must be what
it comes down to: a kid is the road not taken,
      the self that has another chance
   and gets it all right – but no one could really

conceive of that bleary pensioner on TV
as a man who'd got anything right. The shock was
      mortal: might we fail our own past?
   That kid who watched for the cop at a corner

with Chaplin, that nipper who promised a life of
vitality, humour and love, seemed terribly
        (simply by wearing his cap) a
    betrayal of all that might have been if the

film had unreeled in ideal perfection. And
suddenly, in the palace of silent movies,
        we saw the kids we'd been ourselves
    surviving in gestures – jerking, dated, quaint.

They never speak to us, those kids. They scarcely seem
to know that we are what they have become. Always
        they're looking for someone else, and
    though they reach out they can never hold our hand.

Eating Strawberries in the Necropolis

Suppose I had ridden
naked in the Garden in the cavalcade of men
astride a sardonic gryphon, driving the roads
that wove among the dusty olive groves
and coming out on the final commanding miles
across the straight to Carmona, my companions
jouncing on leopards and dromedaries and stallions,
chimaeras and unicorns, into an afternoon sun
hung low on the blinding horizon, under
the hieratic frown of stork and peacock,
metallic dazzles flashing off the trucks,
my thighs hot on the creature's flanks
as I drove the Roman road to the rock
where Man had watched, lord of the wilderness.

Suppose I had ridden
naked all night in the Garden of Delights,
ridden around the water where the women
parleyed with ravens and egrets, ridden
till morning stood like a tree at the window.
And, waking, wanted you.

What else would I do
but walk to the poppied necropolis and sit
on a wall in the shade of the cypresses,
eating strawberries from a paper bag.

The flesh was tender, red as cactusflower.
The juices bled to stain the imperial dust.

Windowless Monads

See how the houses crowd about
the skirts of the hennish church like chickens:
so cosy and close to God,

the comfortable homes of happy families.
Firewood is tidily stacked in the dry;
the axe lies in the dust, a shine

blazing from the blade. Being
may be a bright coincidence; our words
are not the language of things; our smiles

are smiles we have learnt from photographs.
Put up your hair, my love. The nape of your neck
is the home of closeness to me. See

how waiters run to the woman in fox and gauze,
see how the coffee steams, how the cream is white,
see the labour of cake that man has created.

These things must give us pause. Even
a pavement cafe can tell us about our lives;
even a coffee cup includes our love.

Put up your hair and join me, come
and join me out on our balcony of time.
The sun has turned to thunder: but do not

be afraid, it has always been like this,
the waiters watching the coffee cups fill with rain,
the cake disintegrating gracefully.

Tangle

Led on and then abandoned by a
blindness: taking the trains and travelling
light, trusting wire with words

that carry my luggage of love, and ending
the dull unsimple anomie here
in the quiet dark of the city of Mark,

knowing that all my life is in
this anoetic ravelling in the heart,
this harder beat in the throat: no,

you are right, of course, of course you are right,
there must be more to us than love. Although
I like my life enough to want to love you.

Across the shining black lagoon
acataleptic vaporettos ply
like thoughts across the surface of the mind,

exempla of a true hypothesis
I do not even care to try to prove.
I am happiest knowing I cannot know,

breathing the deep sea tang and beating
back the tears and brushing the hair from your face,
not even caring I cannot prove my love:

the rest is canals and the nasty madness
of passages and alleyways and night,
the abject tangle of an Aschenbach.

Adultery

I

There's my presbyterian attitude
to deal with, and your honest heart.

I have been lying here, my cheek
against your breast, remembering

a French corvette that lay on Lake
Ontario, grey in the bright

of a starry night, fingers of light
unclenching tenderly across

the black and fractured gentleness of water.
Hold me. Every love has the government it

deserves. Our parliament is hung,
our members are corrupt.

You didn't warm your instrument
you told your gynaecologist, he said

I did my best, you said
Be gentle, I'm upset. My husband

wants to have children, I don't think I even
love him. I remember

two men looking into a station wagon:
Isn't she a dandy? In the back

a dead doe, bundled on a sheet of plastic,
lay in sticky blood, her belly slit.

II

No guarantees. No promises. No hope.
In the long run I'll do what's best for me.

You talk about your island at Parry Sound
and swimming naked in the sheath of cold,

about the Tina Turner wig
you bought on Yonge at Hallowe'en.

All talk. *I need you. Hold me.* Every love
could do with a reminder of Colbert:

picture us in the forest of Tronçais,
where oaks grown straight three hundred years

thrash their crowns in the topmost air,
each one intended for a mast.

What you see dappling the earth with shade
is the sadness of the rational dream,

the pathos and the pity of the past:
the oaks were planted in 1670 and

matured in the nineteenth century,
when shipping changed to steam.

An Aluminium Casket Would Be a Good Idea

I

My friend Deedee, who is clever and bitter, whose
husband paddled away one day in a canoe,

said she is only having female pallbearers
(dressed, she thinks, in Anne Klein black).

Shelda said there were too many stairs
at Lady of Sorrows, so Deedee said

it could be at All Saints
and Shelda said there was no parking.

I dreamt of my first husband last night.
First time ever. He had put on too much weight

and wanted to give our marriage another try.
I was revolted, but for some reason

he seemed to be living in the same house.
I don't like myself right now. Slack.

Women don't like getting older.
They switch to 15 watt bulbs

(I need a flashlight to get around in here),
wear gloves so they don't look at their hands

on the steering wheel, and stop using
the rear view mirror so they don't catch

a glimpse of themselves. I told Deedee
an aluminium casket

would be a good idea. Karen said
Why don't you just go out and get

yourself a horse, and forget everything.
We drank too much wine, and watched

Anne of Green Gables, a beautiful TV
production, we were all weeping and

a little drunk. All I have ever wanted
for anyone is happiness. And my freedom.

     II

Most of it you probably can guess.
My father used to listen to the news

on CFRB, usually in the driveway in his car.
He was so much like clockwork

he would arrive home at 5.50
and listen to the news before getting out

of his car. My father was strict, small,
he used to work out the horses at

the racetrack as a kid. He had his own
car dealership, and sold it at the right time,

and got into boats, bringing up
the slickcraft from Chicago. I was his.

I foxhunted with him and went to horse shows
and won the occasional ribbon. He kept

an eye on me all the time.
I went to private school, wore a kilt,

was a prefect and drove a yellow Triumph
convertible and was hard on the boys I dated.

He didn't much approve of either marriage.
Just before my father became a

management problem (wandering, pissing)
we took him for an assessment.

He couldn't name my children or make small change.
He knew the prime minister, though;

even at his worst he had political views.
Then he got sick, Alzheimer's, and lost his mind.

I love you now. I dreamt of you.
I was trying to clean myself with wet toilet paper

and it was spit-balling all over the place,
and I heard you pick up some keys

and I thought you were leaving the room
so I dashed out not worrying about anything.

Easter Sunday Deedee sat on a rock
for five whole hours and did not call

her rat of an awful father, for the first time in her life.
Just sat there.

III

Jack tore the fucking fireplace apart
last week for a cool $1000

to fix a smoking problem and has now
created the smoking problem on the second floor.

Do you know, I can have most things I want *if I ask.*
Just like being with my father. Dollar by dollar.

In the long run Jack has always done either
what is right or what I've wanted.

His mother is a monarchist. She lives
in her husband's family home, and has never been

more than fifteen miles from Collingwood.
The family home was built in 1890.

The curtains have hung since 1890.
It's truly original. Stains and all.

Pictures of the Queen, and Winston Churchill.
The Illustrated London News.

Multicoloured towels in the upstairs bathroom.
Bathtub peeling so badly you're scared of lockjaw.

Jack was furious, frightened, wouldn't
allow me to have the child. I was in

my thirteenth week when I found out I was pregnant.
I went to Hampstead, New York. A cattle line-up.

The doctor prodded me carelessly.
This one's saline. I said *Forget it.*

He said okay, he'd do a D & C,
and of course it wasn't complete, I was too far.

They couldn't stop the bleeding.
Does our life only teach us to think things through

and act responsibly? When I came back
from Belgium, I brought some Gueuze for Jack,

it double ferments, he wouldn't drink it
because it was milky. All the time the cork

kept trying to come out on the plane.

The Evidence of Things not Seen

Georgian Bay, Ontario

Jagged jack-pine characters
snagged like battered parasols

building unbuilding in the shimmering
shining westward on the lake:

There's nothing there. Examining
the weaving air: *We're always getting*

ready to live, but never living.
Happiness. The beautiful illusions.

And love has shot a shuttle
through the weft of light and water,

holding close as faith:
living further into the fertile

shifting of the shaping air,
certain of everything we haven't seen.

Concentrating

Standing at the
window watching

three Italian
women rowing,

rocking and tipping and
bobbing, I hear

their laughter find
its natural level

like water. Stay.
Take a look.

Don't you agree,
the flyaway girl

in the cherry cloche
looks like Zelda Fitzgerald?

I'd wave to her
but both my hands

are occupied
unbuttoning your blouse.

Carnation, Lily, Lily, Rose

after John Singer Sargent

Of the several answers to darkness, better than sleep
and lovelier is the lighting of lanterns in gardens,
the claustrophiliac revelation of closeness, light
laden with intimate comfort: important harmony!
        Two girls in white

inhabit this acquiescent tenderness, Alices
cool in Marian shifts, innocents lavender-scented
and cotton-stockinged – you think of Betjeman's bicycle-
riding Oxford girls, the avuncular arousal these
        slim-limbed little

women trigger. What kind of Eden *is* this, anyway,
where only emblematic flowers grow? – carnations for the
experience of blood, lilies for virginity, and
roses modest and flushed (Lolitadom of girlhood!) like
        laundered bloodstained

linen. They are not girls but ideas of girls, and in
the otherworld of intimate green already their thoughts
are of leaving their paradise, as women in Watteau
dream of flying: see, it is in their serious faces
        taking the glow.

Young Mother

      Mother-
        hood having surprised her
   with the same stark shock as rape, she
tightens a white-knuckled hand on each knee
    and balances the small
        ball

      of young
       body in her lap. Long
   lives before and after are blessed
by this sweet violation: for the rest
   of her life she will be
       we.

La Gazzetta

First violin yawns; why,
    he wonders, play
    this crap, when I
could be out having a wild time. Away

    they go: the overture.
    Ah, Lisetta,
    we read of your
talents . . . ('hem) . . . virtues in the Gazzetta.

    A paradigm! And I'm
    tired, he thinks, of
    wasting my time
the same way every day. They speak of love,

    inevitably, and
    Lisetta gives
    at last her hand
to the innkeeper, and we know she lives

    with him without discord.
    Of course! Splendid!
    And we applaud.
How else could life's beginning be ended?

    First violin will go
    home on the tram
    after the show,
incanting to himself: I am, I am . . .

    And we . . .? will do the same,
    afraid to call
    ourselves by name,
for after definition comes the fall.

Silver Wedding

Her smile is his inquisitor.
He cannot think what it might be,
the required answer.

They learnt their disenchantment in their dreams.
Sleep does for everyone, sooner or later:
affection, like Uranus, is castrated.

Love was an annunciation,
an angel delivering messages for a god
they weren't even sure they believed in.

Their hearts are condemned
houses, hurting
for occupation.

An American Murder

for Keith Botsford

Where does the story begin? With the CBS crew
shooting footage for shocker shlock and slavering
       over their cameras as the
   bloodied Bostonian writhed in the driver's

seat by the gargling mess of his dying wife? Or half
an hour before, the Toyota pulled over, his
       finger cocked on the trigger, dull
   disbelief in the eyes of the horsy girl

he'd met at the Gourmet Club, the girl he'd installed in
a life of jacuzzis and pools and insurance?
       Somewhere in the nightmare there must
   be a dream. The dream that a man might have dreamt

who worked as the manager of a furrier store
on Newbury Street. The dream of a boy called Chuck.
       A boy who liked Paris, baseball,
   parties at Bill's. A boy who'd been to school at

the Immaculate Conception. The dream of a man
who'd check into the Sheraton Tara Hotel
       for his last night alive, a man
   who'd be hauled out of Boston harbour under

Tobin Bridge the next morning, leaving a letter on
Tara paper expressing regret for the
       trouble he'd caused everybody
   and saying he couldn't go on. The trouble?

No more than the usual trouble. The usual niggers
arrested. The usual panic in Boston's
       suburbs where whites could understand
   a man who would fill his house with foodie books.

No more than the usual Ave Maria and
tears at the funeral when Chuck's farewell was read,
    beginning *Goodnight, sweet wife.* No
    more than the usual murder. And after

the killing and lying he went to an agent's and
booked a Winter Getaway, never supposing
    that winter was forever and
    was colder than he'd believed in his coldest dreams.

V Lights

A Sonnet

– Write me a sonnet.

                                – What, in half an hour?

– And, while you're at it, finish *Edwin Drood*
and Schubert's Eighth, build me a better Tower
of Babel, put a pleasant attitude
into an Adolf, Slobodan or Pol,
reveal the merely human to the Pope,
get Boadicea playing with a doll
or Albert Einstein watching TV soap,
bring peace to Belfast and Jerusalem,
teach modesty to US politicians,
make people want to live in Birmingham,
and dream up six new sexual positions.

– If trifles such as these can please you, dear,
I'll add a thirteenth month to every year.

The Yuppie in Love

with apologies to Waller

Send her a fax.
Tell her that wastes her time and mine
        that income tax
is fine, bank managers divine,
compared. Say that's the bottom line.

        Say I'd prefer
an increase in the mortgage rate
        to loving her
and being told I have to wait.
For what? To sleep with her estate?

        Tell her I said
I'd rather sell out to the Nips
        than go to bed
knowing she's privatized her lips
and won't be giving any tips.

        Invest your breath
in talk of how she's looking well.
        Then mention death.
And let her name her price. I'd sell
all hell to have that mademoiselle.

To His Coy Mistress

with apologies to Marvell

Had we but world enough and time,
this coyness, lady, were no crime;
but as it is we'll soon be dead,
so cut the crap and come to bed.

The Sigh

from the German of Christian Morgenstern

A sigh went out skating, alone and at night.
He cut a fine figure, but oh! he was frantic.
The moon it was shining, the snow it was white,
and the sigh, the sigh felt romantic.

The sigh remembered a beautiful wench.
His thoughts became hot. Full Fahrenheit hot.
I dare not describe them, not even in French.
And so the ice melted. He drowned on the spot.

There's Something About a Cow

a birthday poem for K. K.

There's something about a cow.
E.g. she has two horns.
She never yawns
to show she's bored.
She keeps a hoard
of extremely old
pirate gold
inside her udder
or under her rudder
(I'm never sure which).
She can jump a ditch
like a steeplechase horse
on the Newmarket course,
she'll dig a well
and cast a bell
and build a bridge
and mend the fridge
and write a dainty Petrarchan sonnet
and fix a frill on your Easter bonnet
and discover a cure for the common cold
(and all, don't forget, with that pirate gold
stashed into her udder –
or under her rudder)
and then after breakfast she'll write a thesis
comparing the soft and silky fleeces
of ancient Arcadian sheep
with the carburettor of a jeep
(a pretty short thesis, it has to be faced).
She has a wasp waist
and she bobs her hair
and she'll never stare
or pick her nose
or publicly manicure her toes –
and, talking of toes, the very best yet

is to see her performing a pirouette
in a tutu and tights
and a shimmer of lights
and then taking a modest and elegant bow
with all of the grace that becometh a cow.
Well, anyhow,
I guess you've got the idea by now:
there's something about a cow.

Stopping by Woods Without a Map

with apologies to Frost

Whose woods these are I've no idea.
His house is miles away from here.
I wonder should I clear the snow.
My horse replies *No bloody fear.*

My horse decides it's time to go.
He's got a watch. He ought to know.
I wonder should I sweep the lake.
My horse replies *Sweet Jesus, no.*

My horse tries hard to stay awake.
He gives his dick a little shake.
I say we ought to get to bed.
We? says my horse. *Eh? Some mistake.*

My smartarse horse will not be fed
nor will I rest my weary head
unless we find the *A to Z,*
unless we find the *A to Z.*

The Essential Auden

I NIGHT MAIL

This is the night mail. Chuff chuff chuff.
Bringing the letters, bills and stuff.
Nice news for some, for others rough.
Uphill the going's getting tough.
This is the night mail. Chuff chuff chuff.

II SPAIN

History will say to the defeated:
Beat it.
Then he'll ask the winner
round to dinner.

III MUSÉE DES BEAUX ARTS

About suffering they were always right,
those know-it-alls. How well they understood dogs
and horses with an itch and kids out skating
and all those reverent passionate old folk waiting
to fall off logs.

How acutely they saw that man was not made for flight!
How well they knew the attempt would end in thrashing
legs, a gurgle or two, a little splashing,
and, centuries later, a bloke with a poem to write.

IV IN MEMORY OF W. B. YEATS

You were silly.
Like us, Billy.

V In Praise of Limestone

Dear, I know nothing of either, but when I try
to imagine a faultless love or the life to come,
what I see is a limestone landscape – that,
or Chester Kallman's bum.

A Treatise on the Astrolabe

Brillig again. The slithy toves
are buggering the borogoves.
They shoot the bolt. They lift the latch.
They bang and bander at the snatch.
They gyre and number with the raths
in every coupling known to maths.
The men have worn their members numb.
The women burble as they come.
The boys and girls are out to play
their frabjous games. Callooh. Callay.

Maud Constance Mealbury lies back.
The watcher's eyes go snicker-snack.
He stands awhile in uffish thought,
his thinking vorpalling to nought.
He jabbers, and her beggar shift
falls open in a wocky rift.
He snaps the shutter on the box.

Her flesh is heir to natural shocks.

The image whiffles in his head,
developing. Though God is dead,
a gimbling virgin logic guides
this mimsy course among the brides,
taking the tulgey woodland paths
across the country of the raths –
contriving by love's astrolabe
to plant his footsteps in the wabe.

The Thunder and Lightning Poker

God's brooding. God is in a mood.
The umbrage of His solitude
clouds up the countenance divine,
like time that ripens in the vine
to swell the darkness of the wine.

God's anger pressures to the quick.
Like Blofeld in a James Bond flick
He burrs His puss and pleasures her,
raising the static in her fur
until the very air's a purr.

God's ardour pulses hard and thick.
Impatient. Throbbing. God's a prick.
He thunders in the dark He's made.
He thunders to be blown or laid.
He thunders for the chambermaid.

God doesn't like to have to wait.
He'll roar and rampage and create.
And regularly, true to form,
He'll sow creation on the storm
to keep His upstairs downstairs warm.

He thunders in a voice of doom
and clumps about His lumber room.
She's there. His appetite's a whip.
He crackles with a jagged rip.
Forgets His manners. And the zip.

And tears the fabric of her dress,
an owner anxious to possess.
Against the wardrobe with a thump:
she thinks, *what now? A standing hump?
Don't gentlemen prefer the rump?*

She's heard them say, last time the Master'd
fathered forth another bastard
He sent the boy to be a Yid
and sold him out for thirty quid.
He didn't seem to like the kid.

She's heard that He's an animal.
She's heard that He's insatiable.
They say no lust will rage as His'll –
that a downpour, not a drizzle,
splashes from His mighty pizzle.

They say His lust takes many guises,
borrows endless shapes and sizes –
a bull or goat, a dove or swan.
It sounds a kind of farmyard con.
And always, once He's come, He's gone.

He forces Mary to her knees,
Lucrece, or Leda, who you please.
Fact is, she wouldn't mind a fuck,
a tumble in the farmyard muck,
a proper service. No such luck.

His juice is sudden. Like a sneeze.
So much, she thinks, for deities.
After the thunder and alarm,
after the storm, a piggy calm
pervades the master of the farm.

No second coming is in sight.
The darkness thickens into night.
The story of the virgin birth,
the handmaid thinks, for what it's worth,
was rigged when farmers ruled the earth,

who must have known that life is force
and rape the first and final cause.
The wrecker with the rampant rod
sows peas in every waiting pod:
the rapist in the garden, God.

The Death of Dracula

a song from Aids: The Musical

The poor Transylvanian is dead,
that lay with the little baggage.
Pericles IV, 2

The Transylvanian is dead.
    That's too bad.
A crucifix above the bed
and garlic wreathed about his head –
    what a lad.

The Transylvanian's deceased.
    Such a shame.
Invite the neighbours to the feast.
We'll have a party for the beast.
    What a game.

His last words (says the nurse) were: *Damn*
    Bram Stoker.
The doctor claims he said: *Fuck Bram.*
Bram sucks. I suck. Therefore I am.
    Some joker.

You're sure there isn't some mistake?
    This *is* death?
I wish we'd brought a bloody stake.
Just keep your speeches for the wake.
    Save your breath.

It's true he's looking rather grey.
    Almost blue.
He doesn't look himself today.
Off-colour. Yes, he's dead, I'd say.
    Wouldn't you?

So even Dracula got Aids.
    I never.
The fiend who bled a thousand maids
has joined the dark Satanic shades.
    For ever.

Even Count Dracula could die.
    Fancy that.
He doesn't look too spruce or spry.
Oh Lord, I think I'm going to cry.
    For a bat.

I never knew the Count *could* kick
    the bucket.
They tell me he was really sick.
They do say: once you've sunk your prick,
    you're suckered.

Poetic justic, eh? King Lear
and that. You long for what you fear.
Let's go. He'd laugh to see us here,
    all weeping.
We'll leave him dead upon his bier.
    (Or sleeping.)

The Critics Are Too Much With Us
with apologies to Wordsworth

The world is full of fuckwits. Sooner or later,
whether you like it or not, they'll lay waste your head.
Whatever you set out to say, they'll say it's been said –
by Lacan, Derrida, Steiner, Allen Tate or
even Eliot, Saintsbury, Walter Pater,
Arnold, or else those Greek blokes – hordes of dead
(or good-as) thinkers in their well-made bed
of critical rigour. God, I'd rather date a
baboon with halitosis and the pox
than deconstruct the mindless bloody farce
of academics getting off their rocks
on isms that enable them to parse
the horseshit of some *nouveau* orthodox
who doesn't know his discourse from his *ars*.

Notes

'Fornicating and Reading the Papers': according to Camus' *The Fall*, this is the sum of what modern man does.

'Homo Sum': a response to Günter Kunert's poem 'Atlantis', in *Fremd daheim* (Hanser, Munich and Vienna, 1990).

'That Christmas': the poem is based on a passage in Captain Sir Edward Hulse's *Letters from the English Front in France*, excerpted in Max Hastings (ed.): *The Oxford Book of Military Anecdotes*.

'Village Performance': the painting by Wang Li-Ping which prompted this poem was reproduced in the periodical *Chinese Literature* in 1977.

'Mother of Battles': the framework of the poem is supplied by the Sumerian myth of Inanna's descent to the underworld. The distinction between Ishtar (Babylonian goddess of love and war) and Inanna (lady of the date clusters, of the granary and byre, of the fertile earth) is blurred in the poem, and the figure also overlaps with that of a Sergeant Susan Kyle whose photograph appeared in a newspaper in the opening days of February 1991, looking down the barrel of her M-16, walkman headphones on her ears, a bottle of Evian water beside her. Other details in the poem (unnamed US Marines dancing the unexplained Gas Mask Dance, Sergeant Robert Brinkofski pictured with his M-60 and sousaphone) also derived from press photos, as did the herdsman of the Inanna myth, unnamed here in tribute to a herdsman photographed during the war sheltering a goat in a sandstorm. I do not believe that to interpret the Gulf War through Sumerian myth is to retreat from political fact or to resign in the face of eternity. It is to insist that, while the anthropologically significant details may vary, the contour of human experience is a terrible constant. Without that recognition we can only go on repeating history. I have no optimism on this score, and believe that that is precisely what we shall do. The herdsman is not a messianic redeemer. There are no redeemers.

'Refugees': the "photograph of war" described in this poem was taken by Robert Capa near Wesel in Germany on 23 March, 1945.

'On Location': one day in the early summer of 1981 I left my office at the university of Eichstätt in Bavaria, where I was then teaching, and came across the scene described here on the square before the cathedral. At the time I didn't recognise the director under his visor and behind his megaphone, and the film plot given in the poem is an invention; in fact he was Rainer Werner Fassbinder and the movie in the making was *Lola*.

'Festival of Youth': one evening in the summer of 1979 I crossed into East Berlin with Timothy Garton Ash, who had begun his career as an observer of eastern Europe with reports for *The Spectator*, to hear Erich Honecker address the annual rally of the Freie Deutsche Jugend. A conversation with one youngster yielded this poem; I've often wondered what's become of him.

'To Gottlob Fabian': Gottlob Fabian was one of my German forefathers, the remotest I am aware of. Since the poem written to him deliberately moves upon sensitive territory, I should state that my awareness of his existence comes from an *Ahnenpass* (Third Reich documentation of "Aryan" ancestry) which until her death was in my maternal grandmother's possession.

'Five Poems after Winslow Homer': in these poems on the loss of faith, written after paintings by the American artist Winslow Homer, I have twice used structural models; 'The Fox Hunt' follows Ted Hughes' 'The Thought-Fox', and 'Kissing the Moon' follows the later version of Goethe's 'An den Mond'.

'Horns': the Hebrew word used to describe Moses at Sinai could mean either "radiant" or "horned", and St. Jerome, in preparing the Latin Vulgate translation, opted for "cornuta", i.e. horned. Throughout the Middle Ages and Renaissance, Moses was therefore represented with horns in art; Michelangelo's sculpture is one of countless examples. This was long considered one of the most celebrated of mistranslations, and on that understanding I wrote this poem; but an American scholar's research has shown that an ancient tradition existed of depicting deities or rulers (Hammurabi, Alexander the Great) with horns as a symbol of their exalted status; and Jerome, aware of this tradition and inferring that the text intended to distinguish Moses in this way, may have interpreted and translated the passage in a symbolic sense, and may have been right to do so.

'An American Murder': for this poem I helped myself to details of the Stuart murder case as reported in *The Independent* (13 January 1990). Charles Stuart shot his pregnant wife in the head and himself in the groin, invented a black assailant, stood by as a black suspect was arrested for the murder, collected a first insurance pay-off, began to make new plans, and finally killed himself, when his brother revealed the facts of the case. (By coincidence the article from which I took the information was written by the novelist and editor Keith Botsford, with whom I subsequently struck up a friendship.)

'Stopping by Woods without a Map': Karl Stead suggested emending the last line to read "or ask the way of C. K. Stead".

'A Treatise on the Astrolabe': Maud Constance Mealbury was one of the young girls photographed semi-nude by Charles Lutwidge Dodgson (Lewis Carroll).

Printed in the United Kingdom
by Lightning Source UK Ltd.
1439